A New True Book

THE PHILIPPINES

By Emilie U. Lepthien

Flag of the Philippines

CHILDRENS PRESS®
CHICAGO

Colorful woven mats are a
specialty of Filipino craftworkers.

AP/Wide World Photos, Inc.—8 (2 photos), 25, 37
(2 photos), 39 (2 photos)

Bureau of Printing and Engraving—23 (left)

© Cameramann International, Ltd.—9, 14 (2
photos), 16 (2 photos), 43

H. Armstrong Roberts, Inc.—23 (right); © Charles
Phelps Cushing, 21

Hillstrom Stock Photos—© Fred Livingston, Jr., 30;
© Jack Lund, 35 (right)

© Emilie Lepthien—6, 34, 35 (left)

Odyssey/Frerck/Chicago—© Robert Frerck, 2, 13,
31, 33, 44

Gladys J. Peterson—15 (left)

Philippine Office of Tourism—28 (left)

Photri—17 (left), 27, 41

© Ann Purcell—45 (bottom left)

© Carl Purcell—15 (right), 45 (top right)

Root Resources—© Lynn Funkhouser, 17 (right),
45 (bottom right); © James P. Young, 45 (top left)

SuperStock International, Inc.—© P. & R. Manley,
Cover; © W. Woodworth, Cover Inset, 4 (left), 11
(right), 28 (right); © S. Vidler, 11 (left), 18;
© G. Ricatto, 29 (left)

Tony Stone Images—© Paul Chesley, 4 (right)

Valan—© Christine Osborne, 29 (right)

Grolier Incorporated—5 (map)

Cover: rice terraces in Banaue

Cover Inset: Two children

Project Editor: Fran Dyra
Design: Margrit Fiddle

Library of Congress Cataloging-in-Publication Data

Lepthien, Emilie U. (Emilie Utteg)
  The Philippines / by Emilie U. Lepthien.
    p.   cm. — (A New true book)
  Includes index.
  Summary: Introduces the country formed by 7,000
islands which stretch from Taiwan to Borneo.
  ISBN 0-516-01195-2
  1. Philippines—Juvenile literature.
[1. Philippines.] I. Title. II. Series.
DS655.L43 1993
959.9—dc20   93-15017
                                  CIP
                                  AC

TABLE OF CONTENTS

Canoeing near Catanduanes Island (left). Many of the Philippine islands are small and rocky like this one (right) near Palawan.

A COUNTRY OF ISLANDS

In Southeast Asia, a string of more than 7,000 islands stretches 1,100 miles (1,770 kilometers) from Taiwan to Borneo. They lie in the South China Sea, which is part of the Pacific Ocean.

4

These islands make up the Republic of the Philippines.

The two largest islands are Luzon in the north and Mindanao in the south. Manila, the capital city of the Philippines, is on Luzon. People live on about 1,000 of the islands.

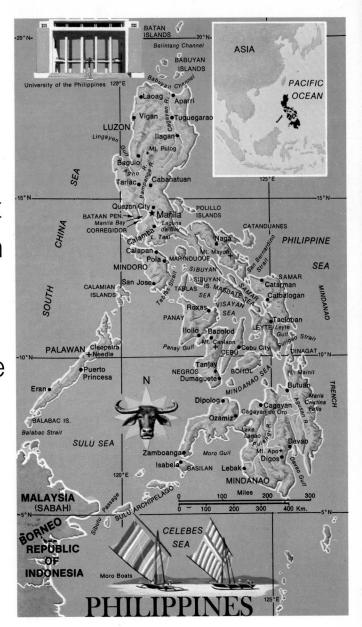

PHILIPPINES

Mayon Volcano on Luzon erupted in September 1984,
and again in February 1993.

RESTLESS LAND

The islands were formed
by volcanoes. About one
hundred of these volcanoes
could still erupt. Mayon
Volcano in southeastern

6

Luzon has erupted many times in this century. Its eruption in February 1993 forced thousands of people to flee the area. Volcanic mud slides also destroyed property.

On June 9, 1991, Mount Pinatubo, about 50 miles (80 kilometers) from Manila, began to erupt. It had not been active for six hundred years. Volcanic ash

A huge cloud of volcanic ash shoots into the sky from Mount
Pinatubo (left) during its June 1991 eruption. Refugees
(right) cross a muddy river as they escape the eruption.

buried hundreds of homes.
The U.S. Clark Air Force
Base, just 10 miles (16
kilometers) from the volcano,
was badly damaged.

The hot and humid climate of the Philippines is perfect for growing tropical fruits. This farm grows pineapples, papayas, and coconuts.

CLIMATE AND WEATHER

The Philippines are in the tropics. The climate is hot and humid in the lowlands. In the mountains north of Manila, it is cooler. At night, the temperature may drop almost to freezing.

9

Rainfall can be heavy. Some parts of Luzon receive up to 216 inches (549 centimeters) of rain a year.

The islands lie in the path of dangerous storms called typhoons. In November 1991, tropical storm Thelma hit several islands. It killed 6,000 people and left 50,000 homeless.

Filipino people:
A man of the
Ifugao tribe (far
left) and a family
group (left)

THE FILIPINO PEOPLE

Most Filipino people are
descendants of Malays
who settled the islands
thousands of years ago.
Today, descendants of
Chinese, Indonesians, Arabs,
Europeans, and Americans
live in the Philippines.

11

About eighty-seven different languages are spoken in the Philippines. In the past, people who settled on different islands could not understand each other. So the government decided on two official languages— Pilipino and English. Pilipino comes from the Tagalog language of Luzon Island. Both languages are taught in the schools.

Fishing boats in the harbor at Puerto Princessa, Palawan Island

The daily life of most Filipinos is determined by where they live. Many who live near the sea work in the fishing industry. They catch tuna, mackerel, grouper, herring, and sardines.

13

Farming in the Philippines: Workers at left are harvesting sugarcane. At right, farmers are transplanting rice in water-covered fields called paddies.

More than fifty percent of Filipinos are farmers, but very few of them own their own land. Most farmers rent land from wealthy landowners.

The major crops are rice, sugarcane, coconuts,

A coconut palm   Carabao plowing a wet rice field

coffee, cacao, and corn
and other vegetables. Most
Filipinos eat rice every day.
    The carabao, or water
buffalo, is the most
important farm animal.
Carabao are used to plow
the rice fields.

15

Logging is also important. Narra, or Philippine mahogany, trees grow in the mountains. Their wood is very valuable.

Many Filipino people are skilled in handicrafts. They

Left: Young girl doing hand embroidery
Above: After an image is carved from wood, a finish is added to preserve it.

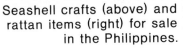
Seashell crafts (above) and
rattan items (right) for sale
in the Philippines.

are noted for their fine
wood carving and beautiful
embroidery. Some islanders
use seashells to make wind
chimes and lamp shades.
Young girls are taught to
weave baskets and mats. **17**

The cross Magellan planted in 1521 is kept in a shrine in Cebu. The wall paintings depict the conversion of the Filipinos to Christianity.

SPANISH RULE

In 1521, Ferdinand Magellan landed on the island of Cebu. He claimed the islands for Spain, and brought Christianity to the people.

Other Spanish explorers soon followed. They called the island chain "Islas Filipinas" for King Philip II of Spain.

For more than 300 years, Spain ruled the Philippines. Spanish officers and the Roman Catholic Church owned most of the land. The Filipino people paid taxes, but they had no voice in the government.

INDEPENDENCE WON AND LOST

In 1891, Dr. José Rizal formed the Philippine League to work for independence. The Spanish called him a traitor and executed him. Rizal's death angered the Filipinos. Led by General Emilio Aguinaldo they revolted against Spain.

In 1898, the United States declared war on Spain. The Americans joined the Filipinos' fight for independence.

The Spanish were eventually defeated. On January 23, 1899, General Aguinaldo declared the Philippines an independent republic.

But now the

Emilio Aguinaldo

United States wanted to govern the Philippines. So, the Filipinos fought the Americans for nearly three years. In 1901, Aguinaldo was captured and the fighting ended. The Americans took over.

The Filipinos still wanted independence. In 1935, a constitution set up the Commonwealth of the Philippines. The United States promised to grant their independence in 1946.

Far left:
President Franklin D.
Roosevelt
Left: General
Douglas MacArthur

WORLD WAR II

The Japanese invaded
the Philippines in December
1941. General Douglas
MacArthur and his small army
of American and Filipino
troops fought, but they could
not stop the Japanese.

In early 1942, President
Franklin D. Roosevelt

23

ordered MacArthur to take
command of all American
forces in the Pacific.
MacArthur had to leave
the Philippines, but he
promised, "I shall return."

On May 7, 1942, the
Philippines surrendered to
the Japanese.

But in October 1944,

General MacArthur (second from left) wades ashore in the Philippines in October 1944.

MacArthur kept his promise and returned with American troops. The Japanese finally surrendered on September 3, 1945. The Philippines, at last, were free.

25

INDEPENDENCE AT LAST

The United States kept its promise. On July 4, 1946, the Filipino flag flew over an independent country—*Republika ng Pilipinas* (the Republic of the Philippines).

The nation adopted a constitution like that of the United States. Elections were held. The first president of the new republic was Manuel A. Roxas.

Buildings damaged by the fighting in World War II

SOLVING PROBLEMS

The Philippines had
suffered great damage
during the war. Although
the Filipinos rebuilt as
quickly as possible, jobs
and housing were scarce.
More and more people

27

Many village houses (above) are still made of bamboo with roofs of thatch. Some city people live in shacks (right) built of scrap materials.

moved to the cities in search of a better life. Most were disappointed.

In rural areas, people lived in small, wooden huts with thatched roofs. In the cities, poor people built shacks out of scrap materials. These shacks

Modern suburbs (left) and a bustling stock exchange (above) are signs of the new prosperity that is coming to the Philippines.

lacked running water, electricity, and other facilities.

In the 1950s, life in the Philippines began to improve. Trade with other countries increased, factories were built, and more jobs were available.

Jeepneys in Manila. Today, new jeepneys are
built in a factory on Luzon Island.

TRANSPORTATION
AND COMMUNICATION

Today, city streets are
crowded with cars, trucks,
buses, and jeepneys. (A
jeepney is a jeep enlarged
for use as a shared taxi.)

The MetroManila LRT (Light Rail Transit), an overhead railway, runs through central Manila. Major airports serve Manila and Cebu. Planes and ships carry people, mail, and goods between the islands.

Rizal Park in downtown Manila

About twenty daily newspapers are published in the Philippines. Most are printed in English. There are twenty-two television channels and many radio stations. The country has one television set for every eight people and one radio for every seven people. In 1988 there was one telephone for every fifty-eight people.

EDUCATION AND RELIGION

Filipinos say that the Spanish gave them their Catholic religion, and Americans gave them their love of education. The law requires all children to attend school through the

An elementary school on Mindanao Island

33

The College of Education at the University of the Philippines

seventh grade. About ninety percent of the people can read and write—the highest percentage in Southeast Asia. There are many universities.

The Philippines is the only Christian country in

The influence of many cultures can be seen in the Muslim mosque (left) and the Chinese cemetery (right).

Asia. Eighty-three percent of the people are Roman Catholic, nine percent are Protestant, and five percent are Muslims. Three percent follow Buddhism and other religions.

PRESIDENTS

Ferdinand Marcos was elected president in 1965, and reelected in 1969. The constitution limited him to two terms. However, Marcos imposed martial law in 1972. In 1973, he announced that a new constitution allowed him to seek a third term.

Under Marcos, newspapers and magazines were censored. People's rights were ignored or denied.

Ferdinand Marcos

Benigno Aquino

Many Filipinos who opposed President Marcos were arrested, including one leader, Benigno Aquino. Finally, Marcos let Aquino go to the United States for surgery.

When Aquino returned in 1983, he was shot and

killed as he left the plane in Manila. Marcos' supporters were accused of the assassination.

Riots broke out. The people wanted democracy. They believed Aquino would have brought back good government.

Many military officers joined in opposing Marcos. Several political parties united in support of Benigno's widow, Corazon Aquino. In 1986, she ran

The people celebrated (left) when Ferdinand Marcos was defeated. President Corazon Aquino (above) promised to make democratic reforms.

for president against Marcos—and won.

Mrs. Aquino's victory forced Marcos and his family to flee to Hawaii. When Marcos died in Hawaii in 1989, the government refused to allow his burial in the Philippines. His wife,

Imelda, returned to
the Philippines in 1991.
She was charged with
the illegal possession of
$10 billion of government
money.

President Aquino tried to
make land reforms. She
survived several coup
attempts by various groups,
including the Communists.

A new constitution was
written under President
Aquino. It limited the
Philippine president to one
six-year term.

President Corazon Aquino with Fidel Ramos

In the May 1992 election, Mrs. Aquino supported General Fidel Ramos for the presidency. In a seven-way race that included Imelda Marcos, Ramos won.

MORE PROBLEMS

In the Philippines today, the New People's Army, a Communist organization, and three Muslim groups oppose the government. In Mindanao and Palawan, armed Muslims have formed the Moro National Liberation Front. They want to establish a separate state.

All military bases previously held by the United States have been

A World War II Pacific War Memorial has been built on Corregidor, an island in Manila Bay. The island was the scene of a last bitter fight between the Japanese army and Filipino and American troops.

abandoned. The Philippine government refused to renew the leases on the bases.

Nevertheless, the United States has continued its financial aid to the Philippines. America and

43

Modern buildings are rising in Manila as
the country becomes more prosperous.

other countries feel that the
new government will last. They
are willing to lend funds to
support land reform and
improve housing. Foreign
businesses will be
encouraged to open

factories in the Philippines.

The people of the Philippines look forward to a better life.

THE FUTURE

The Filipino people are building a new democracy. Their patience and hard work will help them succeed.

WORDS YOU SHOULD KNOW

ash (ASH) — grayish, powdery matter that comes out of a volcano

assassination (uh • sass • ih • NAY • shun) — the killing of a political officeholder or other prominent person

carabao (kahr • uh • BAH • oh) — a water buffalo; an animal that looks like an ox and is used in Southeast Asia as a farm animal

climate (KLYE • mit) — the usual kind of weather and temperature in a certain place

Communists (KAH • myoo • nists) — people who believe in a system of government under which businesses are owned by the state

constitution (kahn • stih • TOO • shun) — a set of rules or laws for the government of a group of people

coup (KOO) — the sudden takeover of a government by a small group

descendant (dih • SEN • dint) — a child, a grandchild, or a person who comes much later in a family line

election (ih • LEK • shun) — the process of voting for people to run the government

embroidery (em • BROY • der • ee) — designs sewn on cloth with colored threads or beads

eruption (ih • RUP • shun) — melted rock, ash, and gases from deep inside the earth bursting out of a volcano

explorer (ex • PLOR • er) — a person who travels to far-off places to learn about the land and the people there

facilities (fuh • SIL • ih • teez) — modern aids to living, such as plumbing and electricity

foreign (FOR • in) — from another country

humid (HYOO • mid) — damp; moist

independence (in • dih • PEN • dints) — freedom from the control of another country or person

jeepney (JEEP • nee) — an enlarged jeep used as a shared taxi in the Philippines

lease (LEESE) — an agreement to pay rent for land or buildings

liberated (LIB • uh • ray • tid) — made free

mahogany (muh • HAW • guh • nee) — a tree with heavy, dark wood

Malays (muh • LAYS) — a group of small, brown-skinned people of Southeast Asia

martial law (MAR • shil LAW) — law administered by military forces

reforms (rih • FORMZ) — changes made to eliminate injustice or wrongdoing on the part of government officials

revolt (rih • VOLT) — to rise up against a government

surrendered (sir • REN • dird) — gave up; admitted defeat

tropical storm (TRAH • pih • kil STORM) — a strong storm with high winds and much rain that occurs in the tropics

tropics (TRAH • pix) — parts of the earth just north and south of the equator

typhoon (ty • FOON) — a very strong tropical storm of the Pacific Ocean, called a "hurricane" in the Atlantic

universities (yoo • nih • VER • sih • teez) — schools of higher learning

volcano (vawl • KAY • no) — an opening in the earth's crust through which material from inside the earth erupts

INDEX

About the Author

Emilie U. Lepthien received her BA and MS degrees and certificate in school administration from Northwestern University. She taught upper-grade science and social studies, wrote and narrated science programs for the Chicago Public Schools' station WBEZ, and was principal in Chicago, Illinois, for twenty years. She received the American Educator's Medal from Freedoms Foundation.

She is a member of Delta Kappa Gamma Society International, Chicago Principals' Association, Illinois Women's Press Association, National Federation of Press Women, and AAUW.

She has written books in the Enchantment of the World, New True Books, and America the Beautiful series.